# MY LIFE AS A PAINTER

**Matthew Sweeney** was born in Lifford, Co. Donegal, Ireland in 1952. He moved to London in 1973 and studied at the Polytechnic of North London and the University of Freiburg. After living in Berlin and Timișoara for some years, he returned to Ireland and now lives in Cork.

His poetry collections include: *A Dream of Maps* (Raven Arts Press, 1981); *A Round House* (1983) and *The Lame Waltzer* (1985) from Allison & Busby / Raven Arts Press; *Blue Shoes* (1989) and *Cacti* (1992) from Secker & Warburg; *The Bridal Suite* (1997), *A Smell of Fish* (2000), *Selected Poems* (2002), *Sanctuary* (2004) and *Black Moon* (2007) from Jonathan Cape; *The Night Post: A Selection* (Salt, 2010); and *Horse Music* (2013), *Inquisition Lane* (2015) and *My Life as a Painter* (2018) from Bloodaxe. *Horse Music* won the inaugural Pigott Poetry Prize in association with Listowel Writers' Week, and was a Poetry Book Society Recommendation. *Black Moon* was shortlisted for the T.S. Eliot Prize and for the *Irish Times* Poetry Now Award. He has also published editions of selected poems in Canada (*Picnic on Ice*, Vehicule Press, 2002) and two translated by Jan Wagner in Germany, *Rosa Milch*, (Berlin Verlag, 2008) and *Hund und Mond* (Hanser Berlin, 2017).

He won a Cholmondeley Award in 1987 and an Arts Council Writers' Award in 1999. He has also published poetry for children, with collections including *The Flying Spring Onion* (1992), *Fatso in the Red Suit* (1995) and *Up on the Roof: New and Selected Poems* (2001). His novels for children include *The Snow Vulture* (1992) and *Fox* (2002). He edited *The New Faber Book of Children's Poems* (2003) and *Walter De la Mare: Poems* (2006) for Faber; co-edited *Emergency Kit: Poems for Strange Times* (Faber, 1996) with Jo Shapcott; and co-wrote *Writing Poetry* (Teach Yourself series, Hodder, 1997) and the novel *Death Comes for the Poets* (Muswell Press, 2012) with John Hartley Williams.

Matthew Sweeney has held residencies at the University of East Anglia and the South Bank Centre in London. He was Poet in Residence at the National Library for the Blind as part of the Poetry Places scheme run by the Poetry Society in London, and writer-in-residence at University College Cork in 2012-13. He is a member of Aosdána.

MATTHEW SWEENEY

# My Life as a Painter

ERIC
BLOO
DAXE

BLOODAXE BOOKS

ISBN: 978 1 78037 414 7

First published 2018 by
Bloodaxe Books Ltd,
Eastburn,
South Park,
Hexham,
Northumberland NE46 1BS.

www.bloodaxebooks.com
For further information about Bloodaxe titles
please visit our website or write to
the above address for a catalogue.

Supported using public funding by
**ARTS COUNCIL
ENGLAND**

Cover design: Neil Astley & Pamela Robertson-Pearce.

Printed in Great Britain by Bell & Bain Limited, Glasgow, Scotland, on
acid-free paper sourced from mills with FSC chain of custody certification.

*to Mary*

# ACKNOWLEDGEMENTS

Acknowledgements are due to the editors of the following publications where versions of some of these poems first appeared: *Ambit, The Dark Horse, The Enchanting Verses, Eyeflash, The High Window, The Irish Times, The New Statesman, The North, Poetry, Poetry and All That Jazz, Poetry Ireland Review, Poetry London, The Poetry Review, Prairie Schooner, Prelude, Reading the Future: New Writing from Ireland Celebrating 250 Years of Hodges Figgis* (Arlen House, 2018), *The Rialto, Southword, The Spectator, The Stinging Fly, Strike Up the Band: Poems for John Lucas at 80* (Plas Gwyn Books, 2017), and *The Well Review.*

# CONTENTS

I am not a painter. I am a poet.
Why? I think I would rather be
A painter, but I am not.

FRANK O'HARA

# The Prayer

When the moon fell out of the sky
I prayed to the sun, like an Inca,
asking the great god to find his pale
godson and bring him back up high
to light up my nights. Streetlights
didn't do it, and never reached the sea
or the mountains, the two terrains that
formed the backdrop to my existence.

I shaped my prayer into a quiet song
that I intoned to a sunflower that
grew in an earthenware pot in my
garden, all the while watched by a black
cat that belonged to my neighbour,
and when I'd finished, the cat and I
watched the moon rise like a football
and regain its rightful place in the sky.

# The Hidden Oasis

Finding the entrance to the hidden oasis
is trickier than winning a race, when blind
and lame, and sleep-deprived for three nights.
It can be done, I know, but only with perverse
willpower. And if you do blunder in, a mad camel
with foul breath will roar at you, sounding like
it's being strangled, but if you kiss it on the lips
it will bow and back away, and you'll smell

the delicate scent of three different gazelle
meats being grilled with fresh thyme, and these
will be served to you with a poached ostrich egg,
palm wine, and flat bread cooked in the sand,
while skilled musicians play the blues on ouds
that lead you to a luminous yellow hammock
where you'll stretch yourself out like a corpse
to dream you're outside, and can't get in.

## Five Yellow Roses

What stopped her bawling was the doorbell
ringing, and a man standing there with five
yellow roses, bulked up with green fronds
and tied in a dinky knot with olive twine.

There was no card to say who the flowers
came from. The man's uniform was blue
with a brown insignia of a spider on his right
top pocket that she saw he kept unbuttoned.

As he waltzed down the path to the gate
the Siamese cat that frequented the garden
raised its back and hissed. The man laughed
and flounced out to his waiting white van.

Oh, the shit-faced side-streets of life! OK,
she'd been born in Madras, in a flowery tea shop
while an albino conjurer magicked a hare
to leap from his heavily ringed brown fingers.

Five yellow roses? Enough to encourage her
to cook saffron rice, with turmeric-tinged prawns
and sautéed yellow courgettes. She didn't play
the Ry Cooder where yellow roses say goodbye.

## No Map

Instead of studying the map any further,
get on your yellow Vespa and fart off
into the forest to bump along that dirt-
track that takes you past the bottomless
lake the twins drowned in a decade ago,
before your bankruptcy, before your
small lottery compensation that lured
the familiar wolves to your black door –
before all of these disturbances, back to
that time you'd whip out the green flute
while drinking wine, and play tunes that
would bring ghosts in from the darkness
to listen, and set the borzoi whimpering
in his sleep – ah, don't think of that now,
get off the bike at the ruined red house
and run past it, up the briar-dotted hill,
at the top of which you'll find a spade –
take hold of this and dig a circular hole
two foot deep, then go round gathering
stones to put in the hole till it's filled up.

# The Fire Devil

The flame jumped onto the newspaper
which flared up, making the old collie
run barking out of the house to where
the ancient farmer was plucking a chicken
in front of the crab-apple tree, and he saw
that feared fire devil dance in the window,
and cursed so loudly the collie ran away,
leaving the farmer to grab a bucket and
limp to an outside tap where he over-filled
the bucket and took it to the back door
to witness the fire devil dancing all over
the cottage – on the chairs and tables,
the curtains, the cupboards, the carpet,
even the doors, making him howl to his
dead wife, his emigrated children but not
to his god who had created this fire devil
and sent him to this cottage to do his dance,
laughing all the while at the sea all around.

# The Parrot's Soliloquy

Birds fly over any border
without being checked,
and do without passports.
We have no photographs
to mark us by, and not even
the hawks are border police
to stop us and send us back.
I speak for all feathered
folk on this matter, watching
you people mass in stations
or slip through razor wire
or suffocate in airless trucks
or drown in the still sea.
I want to tell you about how
the crows and gulls gather
together in yards, or share
electricity cables, or fences.
I want you to imagine the
penguins in Antarctica stood
together in dazed harmony,
even if one marches off alone.
I want to bring in here swifts
who circle the autumn sky,
like wind, communicating
in flat cries, swooping off
together to Morocco, but I
should also mention cages
of quail and wild turtledoves
in the Egyptian markets, or
the ortolan prized in France.
The French, they'd eat me!
We would be fine if you let us
be ourselves, but I am just a
parrot who learned to speak.

# The Nazi Gold Train

The gold-diggers are after the Nazi gold train
on the Polish border, and I'm all for that.
I hope they make a million from it. Such
perseverance in the face of all opposition
has to be applauded. I know the last Nazi-
hunters are baying for reparation to be paid
to Israel, but I don't like the picture in Palestine,
and maybe this is poisoning me. I'm an underdog.
I wish I had Polish ancestry instead of French –
if I had I'd be off to join the gold-diggers, and
I'd claim to be a specialist in dinky gold crosses,
saying they could keep all the coins, and art-
gems, though the latter would be fought over,
I know. Anyway, I'm far from being in Poland,
and I'm flat broke. Maybe this has got me
focussed on the Nazi gold train. Imagine
running all that gold through your fingers.
I once had a hippy neighbour in Donegal,
who tried to tell me riches were dispensable,
but this was abstract. I was broke, even then,
and didn't believe him. I loved the banknotes
I got from the dole. My old red setter, Oscar,
used to roll in them, and I'd take off my shoes
to wade through them. So I could see me,
no bother, breaching a buried Nazi gold train
with an axe and liberating all that good stuff.

# Iceland

I'm out in the garage, throwing mannequins
around, while corpses and blood-puddles
dominate the TV. I need to get away,
but where do I go? I'm hunting my old
childhood globe. I find it under a tricycle,
spin it a few times, and stop at Iceland.
I check the health of my bank balance,
go online, and book a flight to Reykjavik.
I take with me the very minimum – my iPad,
a brand new notebook, Kafka's diaries,
underpants, a few shirts, a stupid sun-hat.
I know very little about where I'm arriving
except I don't know a word of the language,
and I'm not wild about oily fish, and there
are geysers there – although the aluminium
miners may have got to those, I hear.
Anyway, I don't envisage shooters, not
yet. And there's no old, unsorted war,
(apart from that Cod War, but I always
preferred haddock). And the stamps are
cute, in a northern way, and the glacial music
grows on one, even if the cuisine is dodgy.
Still, I settle down here, quite happily, fill
my notebook with drafts of poems that are
bomb-free, bullet-free, and bloodless,
then I look back at the work of the skalds.

# The Hole-up

Lying on your mouth and nose
on the hot sand, you recall
a trip in a boat to the island –
the fat rats that skittered about
after god-knows-what dinner,
the chubby seals staring up,
the sudden realisation that a man
on the run had wintered there
while the soldiers scoured
the entire shoreline to no avail –
you knew now you had been him
out there. You could taste the raw
seagull you'd killed and plucked,
the mussels you'd dug from sand,
the jellyfish that wobbled in your
hands as you slobbered it.
You saw again that first flame
those rubbed stones woke in
the driftwood pile, and that rat
you grilled on a spar and found
delicious. Yes, you'd been that man,
and you had to admit now you
missed that time, that life,
though you were very glad you
had no memory of how it ended.

# The Dance of the Rats

### 1

The gull flew straight at me,
like a bolt from a crossbow.
Just as it approached my face
it rose and veered right, to
the river, where it dived down
and skimmed the water
then zoomed out of sight.

I turned to climb the hill, but
before that, a shirtless man
crossed the road with a woman
to put her in a taxi, and stand
there, waving her away. I knew
then the rats were dancing
in a ring on the grassy riverbank.

I wanted to go and join them,
but I knew I'd scare them away,
so I contented myself with
imagining each with another's
tail in its mouth, and still
squeaks escaping them, making
a music that pleased me hugely.

It had the delicacy of Mozart
as played by ghosts on an under-
water organ, while a downpour
pockmarked the river's surface
like a tight percussion, that
got the crows circling among the
gulls who looked set to attack.

As I rounded the hill the strange
music died away, to be replaced
by the ringing bell of the church,
and I saw a coffin being carried
from a hearse, with teenage girls
weeping loudly as they followed it
through the arched stone door.

I marched quickly on, opening
in my mind the bottle of Malbec
I had lined up to accompany
the chili con carne I had lovingly
prepared that morning, defying
any Texan to better, and I made a
salad dressing as soon as I got inside.


2

Every morning, it seems, a bat
leaves the bedroom just before
I wake. How it gets out through
the closed window (not to mention
the shutters) is beyond me, but
I would pick out that bat from many.
It reminds me of the younger me.

Dates seem right for breakfast,
also maybe figs, and black grapes.
Fortunately, I prefer black coffee –
espresso even, and I like it too much.
I switch off the dark news, though,
and play quiet jazz that meanders
over the table and into my cup.

Yesterday morning, I heard whistling
– quite tuneless, actually, and I
had no idea who was doing it,
but it continued on, making me
anxious, as if something bad was
going to happen to me, not that
I needed signposting for such stuff.

No, the pains come unannounced
in all parts of the body now, as if
the end is being introduced gradually.
Best to turn the music up then, and
maybe open the wine, and yes, let the
white mouse out of its box, forgetting
the small fellow died fifty years ago.

I like to admit things that are past,
as the present seems sometimes lacking.
That outside toilet I used to frequent
up the garden, for example – nowhere
else could I read in such peace, or get
away from everyone. And my dog Bonzo
would lie outside, waiting for me.

This doesn't mean I don't shout for
what is now – for example, me, as I am,
older than I'd like to be, but as my granny
used to quip, *Your backside in a bandbox*.
Yes, and the vegetarian Indian on the
river-bank is worth telling people about.
And the European jazz scene is thriving.

3

I read about a man who longed to eat
the fingers of monkeys, fried with garlic
and wash them down with glasses of piss.
I hope he never realised his desire, but
it's not my concern. I once lived above the
lead guitarist of a punk band – he was
decent and gave me freebies for their gigs.

It seems impossible to have a friendship
with anyone normal – though what is that?
Am I normal? Maybe it goes back to childhood?
I wanted to string a tightrope above the peas
in the garden, and walk it, holding an oar.
I never managed it, and maybe as a result
I'm damaged forever, as regards people.

I think I'm inconvenienced because I can't
sing, like my dad could. Everyone liked him.
He had a nicer smile too, and once I was
told I was not as good-looking as him.
*C'est la vie!* The mirrors are bullies and we
all should throw rocks at them, but then
we'd have to deal with the shards of glass.

I don't know how I'll manage to buy a gun,
nothing major, a handgun. Are there shops
I can walk into and lay a card down, or notes
if that's preferable? I know where I'd practise –
and what target I'd use, with a face drawn
on it in three overlaying colours. Maybe
punk music might be best for those sessions.

Assuming I can acquire the gun, and possibly
a tiger cub, I'd arrive at the victim in late
morning, wearing a crow-mask, and I'd shoot
him point blank in the dead centre of his
forehead, and as he fell, I'd let the tiger
lap his blood. When the Gardaí arrived
with their sirens, I'd try Zen meditation.

And I'd keep my eyes closed as I was driven
away, knowing the rats were out dancing
in a ring that went round so fast, they must
take off. I'd see them so clearly above the roofs
that I'd become one of them, squeaking louder
than any of the others, loving the feel of the
tail in my mouth, and the sensation of flying.

# The Hook

My great granddad lost his right hand
to a tiger. He bought a hook instead,
then he emigrated to Salford to work
on the excavation of the Ship Canal.

Any navvy who laughed at the one-
handed man got the hook in his face,
so scarfaces sat in the Salford bars
every evening and toasted the hookman

who refused to join them because he
didn't like the beer. It had been better
in India. He had his father despatch
cases of his locally infamous poitín

which he slugged alone in his bunk
while reading dark tales by candlelight,
then he'd drink a gallon of tap water
so he'd be right as Mayo rain for work.

My great granddad lost his right hand
but his hook attracted photographs,
and at each snap he extracted a fee
which allowed him to retire at fifty

but he stayed in Salford and opened
a shibeen, which he called *The Hook*,
and he travelled once back to Mayo
for lessons in the making of poitín.

# The Rope Ladder

Climbing the rope ladder in the dark
I had no idea where I was headed,
except up. How far up, I soon began
to ask myself, silencing at the same
time the voice telling me to go down,
as the air around me took on a chill.

Then my spirit itself started to chill
as the wall I rose at vanished in the dark
and I hung there, swinging, looking down
then remembered that I was headed
up somewhere, and it was all the same
what waited for me. As I'd begun

climbing, ordered by my ancestors, I began
laughing, already experiencing a chill,
asking who on earth would do the same,
launch out like this in the pitch-black dark
upwards, not knowing where it headed,
this rope-ladder, that had dropped down

to dangle there, like a hand thrown down
to help me up, and I think I also began
to pray silently, although I'm not headed
to church anyday soon, despite the chill
in my bones, that I imagine is the same
for most of us blundering about in a dark

that's willed and opted for, not this dark
I'm climbing through, switching off the down-
option, going back maybe to where I began,
or forward to where I'll end – just the same,
really, if I'm not inclined to be pig-headed,
and manage to take a zen line on the chill –

but I concede it's hard to cope with the chill
when you climb a rope ladder in the dark
and are so high you forget you started down
there and don't know where you're headed.
Just know this, you're not the one who began
climbing the ladder, even if you look the same.

So learn to deal with the chill, apply the same
discipline to the dark, forget the you that began
far down, and you'll know where you're headed.

# This Life

I saw a black cross floating in the river.
It was one stick lying on top of another
but it was a perfect cross. Then I saw
the shadows of crows on the water,
heading west. Next was a red reflection
of a traffic light – when it turned green
the reflection vanished. And a young man
with a moustache and a black hoodie
ran at me, veering off at the last moment.
I peered at the water, looking for a body.

I decided to carry on, across the bridge,
past the cinema (where the only film I
noticed was a musical). I was tempted by
the Chinese buffet, but resisted, walking
instead into the strategic ambush of a
beggar, which I ignored. What's good
about this life, I muttered to myself, then
recanted. I wanted to get to Iceland –
I'd buy one last lottery ticket, in the hope
I'd get the chance to simmer in a geyser.

# Nazi Dreams

A minuscule filmmaker has set up stall in my head.
He works on his own, with no back-up crew, but
the lighting is always right, and the actor is me,
and the film is always the same, but different.

I'm put in a situation where I'm far from happy –
something has to be cooked in a certain way, against
my normal practice, or the books in the room
have to be organised in a manner I despise

(and that goes for most of the books I shelve).
Or I have to write a poem in a way I never would,
on pain of being pissed on (which sometimes happens)
and sometimes a Luger is pointed at my head.

If I wake up in the night to go to the bathroom
the dream stops, but restarts in another place,
and there I am again, as if the change is irrelevant,
put through my paces in trying to right the situation.

I sometimes want the sleep to hide me, to keep me
from these Nazi dreams, but the Gauleiter always wins
and shoves me back into the impossible situation,
where the only choice is to fight my way to daylight.

# The Lost Wine

*(after Paul Valéry)*


Every single day, under God knows
what sky, I've thrown into the ocean
an offering to nothing – a glass of wine.

Maybe I'm obeying a soothsayer.
Perhaps for the sake of my heart
I dream of blood as I pour the wine.

I love its transparency – it reminds me
of a long-smoked rose, snatched back,
pure, from the currents of the sea.

This wine is lost, the waves are drunk,
and I saw jumping into the bitter air
many faces, all of them profound.

## Schade!

*(in homage to Paula Modersohn-Becker)*


'*Schade!*' she said, as she lay dying,
her baby in her arms. She was 31,
had produced 70 pieces in her last visit
to Paris, was flying to a fame
it would take 100 years to see.
Oh, Paula Modersohn-Becker, you
were ahead of the pack. You painted
yourself nude, the first woman to do that,
neither mother nor lover, a woman.
You showed children looking serious
as stones – the eyes you gave them
had no pupils. I once saw a work
of yours I adored – in Berlin, I think –
it showed a blind woman reaching out
in a wood. I missed it here in Paris today
but I'd rather have your four birch trees
in front of a red house, looking like the
legs of a grey horse you loved to ride,
or your self-portrait with blue irises
against a green background, or your
kneeling girl nude with a stork, than
any other painting I could see in Paris.
Yes, we live turned towards the inside.

# Dialogue with an Artist

## 1  *The Lonely*

*(incorporating the words of L.S. Lowry)*

I used to paint the sea, but never a shore,
and nobody was sailing on it. It wasn't even
the sea, it was just my own loneliness.

It's all there, you know. It's all in the sea.
The battle is there, the inevitability of it all,
the purpose. When I switched to people

they were all lonely. Crowds are the
loneliest thing of all, I say. Every individual
in them is a stranger to everyone else.

I would stand for hours in one spot
and scores of little kids who hadn't had
a wash for weeks would group round me.

Had I not been lonely, none of my work
would have happened. I should not have
done what I've done, or seen what I've seen.

There's something grotesque in me and I
can't help it. I'm drawn to others who are
like that. They're very real people. It's just

I'm attracted to sadness and there are some
very sad things. These people are ghostly
figures. They're my mood, they're myself.

Lately, I started a big self-portrait. I thought
I won't want this thing, no one will, so
I went and turned it into a grotesque head.

You're right, there are grotesques who shine
a dark light that lures us just as the sirens
tried to lure Odysseus, and yes, maybe we
ourselves are among the grotesques, but
there are also the beautiful who, if we're
lucky, save us from ourselves, and validate
the sun's light, and maybe also the moon's.

# Van Gogh's Gun

The beauty had a dragon-tattoo on her foot –
or was it a lizard? – and there were no rips
at the knees of her tight jeans. I sat there,
wondering if Van Gogh would have painted her.

I doubted it. Cypress trees were more his line,
or yellow bedrooms. But those trees quivered,
as if on a computer screen invaded by a virus
and no one could sleep in that yellow bedroom.

Oh, Vincent, as that American singer said, this
world was maybe not for you. But it was, it
was. What else was captured in those paintings
you made – and captured in a way no other

painter has done? You couldn't stick it, though,
and now they're putting your gun on display,
the one that ended your life – not immediately,
your *pistolet à broche* was hardly serious enough

to kill anyone, except you. Vincent, you were 37,
and felt like you'd lived for a century, at least.
I'm not alone in wishing I'd had a drink with you
but a bullet was waiting to tattoo your chest.

# The Blind Clairvoyant

Baba Vanga, I never heard of you.
You were kept secret by Yeltsin.
But I'm learning about you now –
blind, clairvoyant, prophesying this,
that, and everything. You had to get
some things right – the big tsunami,
the melting polar ice caps, the election
of an African-American US President –
but I'm impressed by the prophecy that
two metal birds would attack New York.
I would never have seen that coming.
You stayed quiet on the moon landings,
and the goal-genius of Lionel Messi,
but I did like your insouciant claim
that aliens are living here for decades.
I often imagined this must be the case.
I even wondered if I might be one.
But what's all this stuff about Isis,
and a Europe as we know it being kaput,
replaced by a caliphate, with Rome
at its epicentre, all this in ten short years?
Come off it, Baba Vanga. Admit, from
death, that this was maybe a dumb call,
one of your 20 or 30 percent misfires.

# A Belief in Angels

I met a woman tonight who believes in angels.
She saw my own guardian angel standing behind me,
keeping a hand on my left shoulder. I saw nothing.
I should have asked what he looked like, what colour
his hair was. Yeah, what a missed opportunity!
I did ask her if she'd met other angels. 'Often,' she said,
without any details. Before I pressed her on this,
I asked if my guardian angel minded that I didn't
believe in him. She smiled and said 'No problem' –
he would be waiting for me when I died. 'I see,'
I said, 'but what about some more details of angels?'
'Where should I start?' she asked. 'When I was nine,
an angel came to me at school to tell me my brother
would die. He did, three days later. And then, one
morning, another appeared to tell me I would win
the dance competition. I did, of course. And then
five angels manifested themselves to stand around me
to announce they were bringing me to God, yes,
they said that, and I found myself sitting on God's knee
while he stroked my hair, saying I was his puppet.'
What could I answer to this, I asked myself and decided
nothing. As a heathen, I had no angels to call on.
And I had never been anyone's puppet, or wanted to be.
I took a taxi back up the steep hill to Sunday's Well.

# A Donkey in Dombey Street

I heard a donkey bray in Dombey Street.
I looked around but couldn't lay eyes on him.

The noise went on like someone sawing
a London plane down, a sculptor, possibly,

looking for wood to carve a magnum opus from,
or maybe, like a hanged man left swinging.

What on earth was going on in Dombey Street,
thirteen years after I'd stopped living here?

I went upstairs and stuck my head out the window.
The breeze fluttered the lupins of the facing house

while a drain in the street was fenced off in red.
There was no sound whatsoever to arrest me.

Where was that airhead downstairs neighbour
who'd played hardcore reggae deep into the night,

or those gangs of feral cats that cried till dawn?
The donkey clearly knew all this loud local history.

If I found him we could create a new din together,
so I rummaged till I dislodged my old yellow bandana

and stomped down the stairs, whooping like a Sioux,
to crash out the front door into Dombey Street.

# My Life as a Painter

The three small birds my father brought me
on a plate had been shot by him a week before,
then plucked, gutted and pot-roasted (not by him
but by my grandfather), and my father sat down
opposite me, asking me to sample each, then tell
him which I preferred. One was a snipe, one a
crake, one a wood-pigeon. I tasted them all,
picked out the lead shot, and liked the pigeon.
My father laughed and said it was his least favourite.
Or maybe he claimed to enjoy all the birds equally.

I often find a wish going through me to remake myself
as a painter. Those three birds would be perfect
for my first work. I wouldn't depict my father on
the hill with the shotgun or Rossa, the red setter,
running to collect the birds. No, I'd stay faithful
to the old concept of the still life or, in French,
*nature morte*. Birds on a plate, nothing else.
I might add a few colours that weren't there.
And I'd follow up with a long, flat portrait of three
spectacularly blue-moulded loaves, all of them rye.

# The Man with the Pillow

I saw a man with a pillow
disappear through a gate
metres from the riverbank.

It was opposite the cinema,
and if I'd had a cine camera
I'd have aimed it at him –

It would be the start of a film
that would require an art cinema,
which ours is definitely not.

I'd take him back to when he
was approaching the gate,
the pillow under his left arm.

I'd focus on his face, his eyes
for a long time, like Orson Wells.
I'd have Baltic jazz playing.

Maybe it would be good to hear
a dog barking, not far away.
I'd follow him with the camera

to see who would greet him,
when he rang whatever doorbell –
I wouldn't ask him any questions.

Most likely it would be a woman,
but it could be a man with a monkey
or with an owl on his shoulder.

I'd be open to anything, as a real
artist should be. Yes, I saw my new
career panning out, and it was good.

# Nowhere Man

Halfway up the steep hill, I noticed
a bald-headed young guy standing
on the roof of a yellow Mini-Minor,
singing John Lennon's 'Nowhere Man'.
His accent added a *je-ne-sais-quoi*
to the lyrics. I found myself applauding
before he finished, then racing up
to give him a €10 note, and asking him
to repeat his act, or sing another song,
which he seemed to appreciate greatly,
flashing me a smile I wish I'd captured
on my stupid phone which was on strike.
He swayed on the roof and launched
into my favourite Beatles song, 'In My Life',
making me sit down on the kerb and cry.
How these French men knew how to pick
the best Beatles' songs (always Lennon's)
and sing them so well in that accent was
as bewildering to me as their grammar.
Anyway, I wanted to hop up on the roof
and hug him. He bowed at my reaction,
then jumped down, and disappeared.

# Beggars

The sun brings the beggars out,
as well as the regulars, twice as many
are sitting on the pavements, with
paper cups in front of them. Some
are undecided – one had a mouth-
organ sitting on a cap, and a woman
said she would give him nothing until
he played, so he did, badly, but no
matter. The regulars are annoyed.
One young shark is flashing his eyes
as if to say he's the serious one,
among all these amateurs, and I must
admit I believe he has a point, although
I've passed him a hundred times,
and haven't given him 50c. No,
I haven't even weakened slightly from
my long-time, hard-line stance. Anyway,
I head to the market, buy my organic
rocket leaves and giant radishes, pop in
to the Mutton Lane Inn for a pint, flick
through *The Irish Times*, then trudge off
back up the Sunday's Well Road, where
halfway, I'm overcome, and lie down
on the warm pavement for a snooze,
taking my cap off and laying it down.
I wake up to find 10€37c inside it.

# The Coin

There is a bright coin on the street,
probably a 2€ coin, hopefully a 2€ coin,
but the traffic is relentless, like a river.
Even when the lights stop it, a truck
is over the coin. Should I slide beneath
the body? But these lights aren't red long,
and the driver won't know I'm down there,
under his load of carpets, or chairs, or TVs.
I'm thinking of what I'd buy with the 2€ –
a sausage from the market, with mustard,
or a quarter pound of minced steak and
a small onion, or even half a rye baguette.
But what if it's only a shiny 20c coin?
I'd get nothing with that. No point in
thinking like this, I say to myself, seeing
that a woman has also noticed the coin
and is poised to jump. I glare at her, inching
to the edge of the pavement. So it must
be a 2€ coin, and I must beat her to it,
at the risk of being run down by a bus.
The lights are turning again. I'm a diver
on a board, and I go, as a taxi screeches
to a halt, horn blaring, with further
screeches and wailing, but no smash.
My fingers clutch the 2€ coin, which it is,
while my teeth bare in a grin for the woman
and all the drivers who are scowling at me.
I get to my feet and make for the market.

# The Message

It took him two minutes to realise
the message the boy had brought him
was encrypted. How on earth was he to
read it? Who'd sent it? He held the piece
of black paper up to the sun so the white
lettering shone. It may as well have come
from the moon. He noticed the boy was
sitting on the wall, swinging his legs.
Was he waiting on some kind of a reply?
This was too much pressure for a man
trying to light a barbecue, with guests
due to arrive any minute. He took a swig
of Rioja, as if this would unlock his brain.
The message looked like no language he'd
seen, and nor was it figures, or symbols.
It could have been written by a crow.
The loud laughs of two women arriving
with wine bottles spooked him. What
could he do? The boy was watching him.
Maybe one of his guests could decode
the message. People could surprise one.
Anyway, it was time to see to his guests.
He wondered if the boy was hungry –
he might welcome the offer of a köfte.

# The Thin Brothel

Coming up the hill, you see it – the terrace
facing the river ending in a vee with the sharp
point sliced off, replaced by a huge window
where a big revolving light shines out to lure
the climbers. It's not red but mauve, but still –
the intent is transparent. Yet I've never seen
a lady, scantily clad or otherwise, hanging
about outside the curious-looking building,
or heard any sultry music emanating from it.
Maybe I should head down there at 3 a.m.

And if I did, where would I find the door into
the welcoming room – on the river-facing side,
tucked away from the traffic-busy street?
Should I be ridiculous and bring flowers, or
at least dark chocolates? I'd wear a red tie,
and I think I'd bring my white Labrador puppy
to charm the ladies, if they're there at all.
And you know something, I hope they're not,
as I would have to admit I have no custom for
them, but that man behind me undoubtedly has.

# The Red Helicopter

Who authorised the red helicopter
to fly over the city, and stay
buzzing there, cruising in wide
slow circles, like a giant vulture?

The noise crashed into my sleep
yesterday morning before I knew
what it was, then when I realised,
I looked out and saw nothing

though the blades kept whirring,
getting louder, then quieter, but
never stopping – they wouldn't until
they'd found what they were looking for.

I ducked under them to go into town
to buy the dinner. A cloud emptied
so I taxied home, and heard a search
was on for a sixty-three-year-old man.

I was that man but what had I done?
Had I killed someone and not noticed?
I went into the kitchen, played Coltrane
so loud it silenced the helicopter.

I also attacked the Scottish malt.
This morning the noise whacked me again,
so I ripped the shutters open, and
there it was, big and red in the sky.

It was hovering right above the house.
There was no hiding place any more.
I pulled on my kimono, marched out,
barefoot, onto the terrace, to stand there.

# The Bunker

When the neighbour's TV aerial
snapped off and flew away like a
tiny spaceship, and a toddler
I'd never seen was deposited
by a wind in my garden and ran
away, laughing, I decided to
enquire about second-hand
nuclear bunkers. They block
gamma rays, you see. And the
world was weirding. Anyway,
I was directed to eBay, and sure
enough, found plenty. I opted
for one in Wicklow – an ancient
CND buff on his uppers. Weren't
we all? So, I took three buses
to see him and his bunker.
It was thorough, but untested.
It was also untransportable.
Still, I decided to shell out for it.
He produced sherry and wild
mushroom vol-au-vents. He played
Coltrane's *My Favourite Things*.
I found him altogether agreeable.
A white van arrived from Cork with
me in it, also two shovels, a pickaxe
and a pair of Polish men. Together
we made a lot of noise and dust.
I shook hands with the nice old man,
then the three of us took off
back south, and the guys agreed
to rebuild the bunker in my basement
(they needed to make a few tunnels
but we didn't tell the neighbours)

46

and they did OK. I paid them well.
Most nights now I sleep down here.
I play contemporary European jazz.
My dreams, on the whole, are better.

# Frogman

When the river rose as much as he hoped it would,
and the first wavelets explored Kyrl's Quay
he ran back up the hill to his house, unlocked
the heavy door, took the stairs two at a time, stood
on a chair to rummage on top of the wardrobe till
he got all of his diving suit that he'd secreted there.

Laying it on the bed, he admired it – not black, like
most suits, but dark green (ordered from Russia).
He undressed and got into the drysuit, checking
how he looked in the mirror. He strapped on the
backpack box and stuck his head in the diving mask.
The flippers he'd keep till he was entering the water.

Switching on the TV to see the progress of the flood
he saw it was over-running the city centre. Excellent,
he thought, locking the door and loping down the path.
His neighbour laughed loudly at the sight of him, but
he ignored the man, foregoing his usual greeting.
Minutes later the drivers couldn't look at the road.

Halfway across the shaky bridge he donned his flippers,
hopped up on the parapet and dived in. Two boys
saw the splash and cheered. He swam on, rolling
over quickly to see the stream of bubbles in his wake.
He felt as lean in the water as a combat diver, maybe
he should have brought a knife and a limpet mine.

When he came to the bridge by the Gate cinema
he had no need to climb out. No, he swam over the wall
and down the middle of North Main Street. Cars
were stalled, half-submerged. A young man splashed
alongside him., fully clothed and singing. Ahead
a female Garda was attempting to direct the traffic.

He darted past her, alongside a pair of startled grilse.
Seagulls were circling overhead, as he veered left
to Daunt Square where two men waded with a statue
of the Virgin, trying to get the flood to subside. Yeah!
The water was rising, soon it would be over the roofs.
He looked forward to being the city's last survivor.

# Seagulls

The seagulls in Guernsey had been the Nazis
who'd conquered the island in the 40s, so
easy to explain their take-all diving to snatch
hamburgers, cones, from the child he'd been.

They may even have driven him away, across
the sea to Ireland, where the gulls were smaller,
almost polite, happy to stick to the herring,
and keep a wide berth from humans like him.

He began to half-admire them, and bought
binoculars to study their shrieking aerobatics,
marking them much higher than the crows
that shared these Irish skies with them.

But the gulls began massing on the high-voltage
cables outside his house, and a day came
when one swooped on his dog and carried it away,
with the rest of them flapping loudly in pursuit.

He never saw his dog again, and began to keep
his baby inside, and he revised his hasty opinion
of the gulls, who continued to crowd the cables
as if they were planning a huge avian offensive,

so to ward off any such malign development,
he devised a strategy of defence through attack –
a very old story. He bought ten crusty loaves
and a hundred razor blades, and spent a couple

of hours breaking off chunks, embedding
a razor blade in each, then bagging them all,
driving to the North Mall, and getting out of the car
to stand and empty the bags into the River Lee.

# Colombus on Gomera

### 1

I set out alone by boat this morning to
the western side of the island, the charms
of which were outlined to me last night
in the *taberna* by the lovely Beatriz, who
would know, as we dined on garlicky shrimps
with the utterly peculiar sea cucumber,
and sipped smoky yellow wine – anyway,
my lady told me to get to the Valle Gran Rey
and walk among the undergrowth. So I
did, and attracted by a strident noise,
I interrupted two giant lizards mating.
I wondered if my sweet lady intended this.

### 2

I have stayed too long here because of her.
My ships are repaired from the abundant
forest that crowns this unique island where
mists blot out the trees. I have hired men
to replace my sailors who've absconded to
the company of the local red-haired women,
and I couldn't blame them. Am I not almost
as bad? This morning I went to the church
and bowed to the statue of the Virgin, then
knelt at the altar to ask God's blessing for
the great voyage, across a terrifying ocean –
if I can ever wrench myself free of this lady.

3

I have heard that the shepherds here talk to
each other in a whistle language that can
cross great distances – they call it *El Silbo*.
Maybe I could learn that and whistle to my
love from the new world I know I will find.
Part of me, though, wants to stay forever
in this perfect port of San Sebastián, in my
comfortable lodgings in the *Casa de Colón*,
with its wooden shutters that keep out what
I don't want, and let in what I do, and its
discreet courtyard, bright with greenery,
where I can spend time with whoever I want.

# The North Wind

I carried my three bags down the road from the bus
into the teeth of the north wind. There was a minuscule
polar bear in each gust, and they were biting, biting,
then spitting bits of me out onto the road, where rats
could devour them. I was much smaller when I lugged
the three (rucksack on my right shoulder, laptop bag
on my left, canvas bag of presents in my right hand)
up what we called the *loaning* – a leaf-framed, uphill
lane from the road, but I was still big enough to slip
and fall on wet moss just as I was reaching the house,
after nine hours on trains, trams or buses from Cork,
and my jeans got caked in mud. The north wind blew
into my horizontal face, and I swear, it laughed at me.
I struggled to my feet and gained entry to the house,
dumping my bags inside the door. I recovered a bottle
of rioja from the rucksack, and I uncorked it, filling a glass
to the brim, then bringing this to the re-opened door
before downing it in one slug, ignoring the north wind.

# Google Maps

*(for Nico)*

The Google map on my phone
led me to my daughter, and her two
little ones. It was just like that star
that brought the three boyos
to the baby in Bethlehem. Yeah!
Without it we would have been lost
like wanderers in the desert, with wolves
slinking after them in the moonlight.
And speaking of the moon, that fellow
was up there, thin as a fingernail clipping
(ten of which I produced yesterday)
and his pet bright star was beneath him
like a loyal cocker spaniel, whose
one eye shines out into the night.
I feel I've nearly visited the moon, as I
chatted with a man who's been there.
And if I wanted to retrace his steps
Google Maps would lead me
unerringly to the Sea of Tranquility
or to the nightclubs of the dark side.

# Hey Jude

*(for little Jude)*


When you sing your song
you can make it an angry one,
and do it so loud the punks climb out
of their graves to applaud.
Give them your autograph.

When you buy that submarine,
don't paint it yellow – no, you can
opt for black, and wear a
black eye-patch as you stand
on the conning tower, coming
into the harbour, smiling.

But when you decide you want
a panther, maybe look for a
white one. They're cooler,
and who knows, you could
name your band after it,
adding an S, and get teeshirts
made, so you can clean up.

And what about green hair,
and a green beard? (Don't forget
the eyelashes.) You could try
being a vegan, and if you
play in Chicago on Paddy's Day
they'll ply you with green beer.

You could learn to talk to horses,
or even dogs, but not cats.
Take up a weird variant of zen,
and adapt to speaking Italian,
with a side interest in grappa.

If you stop to think of me at all,
Imagine a brown bear in an office
looking for the way out. Don't
worry, I'll have my own jar of
honey, and I'll be wearing blue
sunglasses and a porkpie hat.
And I'll be whistling a polka
as I blunder down the corridors.

Anyway, I hope you live to be
a hundred and ride a red unicycle
down Kurfürstendamm, cheered on
by thousands, while pink bubbles
float above the Reichstag
and try to get to the moon.

# My Mother's Wine

In my mother's late years she liked her wine,
her red wine. She never touched white,
just as earlier she'd avoided all alcohol, and
objected to anyone drinking it near her.
My father was the same, wearing a Pioneer
Pin to every public event. One evening, over
dinner, I slid in the fact that in France and Italy
wine was considered part of a meal. I see,
he said, and began trying small sups of wine.
My mother followed suit, of course, and soon
was outdoing him, sliding her glass down
to be refilled. Soon the empties began to
accumulate beneath her bed, although the
supplier remained a mystery. Was this after
the Alzheimer's had started to take over?
It was round about then that my brother
began substituting alcohol-free wine,
claiming she wouldn't notice the difference.
Yet, one evening, shortly before she died,
we all ate together, and when my brother left,
she pushed her glass away, asking me to pour
some of my wine, saying she preferred that,
but my brother trumped my recounting of this
by telling me that in a video viewed after mother
had died, she could be clearly seen swapping
her offering for his real dose of wine, so I
raise this humble glass of a passable Bordeaux
to my mother, wishing she were here to join me.

# What Odds

*(for Auntie Nell)*


When the red setter ran up the field
after the sheep, and the farmer
dug out his shotgun, and I ran,
screaming, to drive the dog away
down to the beach and into the sea,
then slunk with him back up the hill
to the big white house, where I
shaved off my beard in a frenzy –
*What odds*, my aunt said, *What odds?*

When the poisonous jellyfish washed
up on the beach, and the Gardaí came
to warn everyone to stay away,
even the windsurfers, who ignored
them, and squelched with their flippers
out to the waves that rose so high
they felt they were free, and children
cried because they couldn't bathe –
*What odds*, my aunt said, *What odds?*

When the helicopter crashed
onto the turfhouse, and the winter's
turf went on fire, and only the
quick-thinking neighbour's attaching
the hose to the outside tap made
inroads enough on the flames to
enable the fire-brigade to douse them
and save the house from inferno –
*What odds*, my aunt said, *What odds?*

When the storm from space struck
and the tsunami savaged the beach
and swarmed up the road to engulf
the big house, sending us all up to
the flat roof above the scullery,
pulling doors off their hinges to float on
when the water rose, and gangs of gulls
swooped low, shrieking, overhead –
*What odds*, my aunt said, *What odds*?

# Donegal

Why is the bin lorry stopped outside the cemetery?
Why is the caravan planted in the middle of the field?
Why is the fleet of buses parked for months in the yard?
Why is the boat upside-down on the side of the hill?

The answer to all these questions is you're in Donegal.
Go out to our islands – make a start with Inishtrahull.
Photograph the dog's tombstone in the tiny graveyard
where most of the other graves have wooden crosses.

Next try Arranmore – observe the wrecked cars in the fields,
then have a drink in any bar, and find it doesn't shut.
Lastly, be good to yourself and take a boat to *Oileán Toraí*.
You'll be met on the pier by the King of the Island

with his accordion, and he'll lead you to his favoured bar
where he'll sink brandies, and pay for none of these.
And he'll produce his naïve paintings for you to peruse, in
the sureness you'll have no option but to purchase one

that he'll sign, then serenade and toast you, after
which you might want to walk out to the lighthouse
under the full moon, followed by the last corncrake.
And you'll feel blessed to have ended up in Donegal.

## Mehh!

Before I could speak properly,
like many tiny twits, I made up my
own words, some of them better
than any I've found in all the lingos
I've sampled. I mean, take this one –
'It's a *mehh*!' Well, I couldn't have
managed the intro words, but I'd
shout '*mehh*'! And I'd point at it,
and back away from it, at speed,
to hide under the biggest cushion
in the house, where I'd quake like
the jellyfish I once saw in the sea,
waiting for the '*mehh*' to float up-
stairs, stretch itself and gobble me.
I should try to translate the word,
but we know how hard translation is.
For example, if I say it was a feather,
the whole terror aspect is lost – who
fears a feather? But the visual aspect
of a '*mehh*' was indeed a feather.
And again, apart from its scariness,
it introduced me to the spin of magic,
and metaphor – how, I don't know,
but whenever I saw a '*mehh*' on
the floor, the world would be hopping,
and suggesting this, that and the other,
not that I could have articulated such stuff
so maybe it was the first sign that
I was meant to become a *makar*, and
I should now make a hat of feathers.

# The Hards

They came from Derry, wore trousers
up to their ankles, had terriers that would
rip your jeans at the back of your legs.

I had a grand-aunt, Marianne, who lived
in Pennyburn, so I spent some days in
Derry, but it didn't endear me to the city.

I remembered that when the boys from
the Lecky Road had a go at me before
they ran down to those beach-houses,

that back then I marvelled at. I mean,
how could cottages be built so close
to the sea, and to the breaking waves?

And why were they invading Ballyliffin?
In our home they were hards, just that.
We were not encouraged to speak to them.

Hards, really, and despite my trying to make
peace on the golf course with the two I ran
into years later, and drank a few pints with,

it's the term that stays because I hear it
still every time I stand on the beach, staring
at those houses I wasn't allowed to enter.

# Lisdoonvarna

Lisdoonvarna, of all places, was where he demanded
I meet him, to hand over the money. Was he pretending
we were going there to each pick up a country lassie
at the Matchmaker's Fair? I asked him how I'd get there.
Take a boat, he said. Very funny, I barked, then hung up.

I went down the hill towards the bus station, passing
a woman with two poodles, one in a push-chair, the other
under her arm. The sun was shining as if it was deluded
we were in Spain. I had Charlie Parker playing merrily
in my head, as I'd just taken off the CD before I departed.

I'd ransacked under the mattress and amassed five grand
which I'd crammed into a football sock. Seemed a lot to me
to apologise to him for giving him three donkeys painted
in black and white stripes, and claiming they were zebras.
I mean, he couldn't claim his pathetic Kerry zoo was great.

And if the weather in Kerry was as good as it was in Cork
the rainstorm wouldn't have washed the stripes off, or made
the donkeys bray. At least, the Gardaí weren't dragged in.
He'd paid me two grand for the three. He was making a profit,
that was fine, but why did I have to travel to Lisdoonvarna?

# Retribution

When I missed an obvious winner at Cheltenham
and had drunk enough wine, I knew I had no option
but to find the black cane in the cupboard, switch on
the outside light, then take myself onto the terrace
where I'd drop my jeans and flagellate myself in full
view of whichever of the neighbours were interested.

It was a Friday night, and they were likely to be hosting
one of their all-night parties, where conversations slipped
through the walls, with minimal music, but even so
I couldn't sleep. I would like to catch their attention
in however unconventional a way, but in a semi-war
situation, all was allowed, was it not? Anyway, I savaged

myself severely enough to interest any young people
who weren't already stoned, or fornicating. I got no
response, of course. I might have been trimming chives
or draining the bay leaf pot. I wanted to turn myself
into a horse and jump into a time-machine, and make
my way to that race I stupidly lost out in at Cheltenham

# Tin Mining

Instead of climbing the wooded hill
you should descend into the tin mine

that hasn't been used for twenty years.
Be sure to take a hard hat with a light

and wear hiking boots. Avoid any
attributes such as belts or braces

that could snag on any rusty metal.
You won't need to bring a canary

for this kind of mine, but bring a small
pickaxe – there's still tin there if you

can locate it. Imagine the homemade
jewellery you'd charm your woman with,

say a brooch with the old three hares
circular motif. Take a bottle of Cornish cider

and a Toby jug with your own face on it
to celebrate – howl out a local folksong,

then climb out to round up some tourists
for the dance called the Tinners' Rabbit

involving sticks and a complex rotation
you'll have to learn and teach the others,

after which you can all retire to Zennor,
and *The Tinners' Arms* to drink more,

shouting out toasts to the Queen and Duke
of Cornwall, and anyone who takes your fancy.

# Wiener

The white dog with the black half-coat
stared at me as I rumbled past in a taxi.
He conveyed his thoughts to me. He wanted
a Wiener, a frankfurter. I asked the driver
to brake, but the man refused. I shook my
head and whistled the Horst Wessel song.
I suddenly wanted a Wiener myself, but
where could I find one in downtown Ottawa?
Yes, three Wiener, with light sauerkraut
*(und Senf)* would be dandy. The banjo players
were blasting away on the improvised stage
in my absence, and women were dancing.
At that, I saw the white dog looking for me –
the walls were transparent, the distance
between us was nullified. He was running
down Elgin Street (or *rue Elgin*), with his
master roaring after him. I was honoured,
and more than a little ashamed. If he ran
down the steps and bounced in here, barking,
I had no Wiener to give him. Would he accept,
as a replacement, a dish of *confit de canard?*
I waited for his telepathic response.

# Quiz

*Two lines crossed above the city of Melbourne –*
which celebrated poem begins with this image?

Who played the Ghost in *The Haunted Menagerie*?
Who played the Moon in *The War of the Galaxy*?

Which minerals are present in the average dog-turd?
What is the name of the colour only seen by fish?

What really happened in the Amelia Earhart mystery
and who was the trailblazing female pilot's navigator?

Where and what exactly was the Lost Colony of Roanoke?
Explain why the Dancing Plague of 1518 is so-called.

If I were to stand on my head and sing, who would I be?
Which are the two words used for a five-legged horse?

In the 1952 FA Cup final, who scored the winning goal?
What animals are drawn on for Quetzalcoatl's symbol?

The owl-hoot is a recurring motif in which symphony?
What was the currency used on the lost island of Atlantis?

# These Colours

*(after Jim Jarmusch)*

The woman with the red shoes
scowled at the one with yellow shoes
as they walked away from the grave.
Above them a green model plane droned.
The priest hurried after them, clucking
but they both gave him no time at all –
no, they were as responsive as peahens.
The plane spluttered and dived into the pond.
A poet sat in a tree recording these happenings,
these colours. He wasn't a painter. He had
a dried sunflower in one buttonhole,
and a dwarf red tulip in the other.
He went to the pond, waded in, and found
the model plane. He sat looking at it
for hours, then he retrieved his notebook
from his purple bag, and resumed his calling.

# The Blue Cabbage

No, I won't cook the blue cabbage,
I'll let it grow so big (with copious
showers of gorilla spit) that I can
take a circular saw and cut a door
into its gnarled interior, where I'll
carve out with a sword a sanctum,
then string up a goatskin hammock,
to recline in, humming star-music,
while pickpockets prowl the streets.

Yes, I'll consider staying in there,
forever, although I might get hungry,
not to mention thirsty, but I could
think of inventing blue sauerkraut,
and blue *schnapps*, using the cut-
out bits of my new home, and I'd
have to consider offering the excess
to strangers – and just maybe I'd
ask them to pay in blue banknotes.

# Mullett Lake Couplets

Is that an elk I see, swimming across the lake,
its huge antlers like sails helping it along?

How come so many fishermen catch nothing?
Are worms extinct in northern Michigan?

Are we far enough up to see the Northern Lights?
I know a bald eagle is nesting in a nearby tree.

I put a ladder against the gable of the cabin,
climbed up, and stretched to touch the moon.

A ghost Chippewa stood smoking on the porch
while I drank wine, pretending not to see him.

Saying *perch* thrice makes one leap into your hands.
A sharp knife will fillet it, and a pan will fry it.

I think I'd prefer a tenderloin of that swimming elk,
I'd marinate it with garlic in Mission Point red wine,

then I'd grill it briefly on a driftwood barbecue,
in the dark, helped by fireflies and a purple candle.

# Black Squirrels

Two black squirrels are dancing on the porch
in a kind of tango. I run for my phone but they
resist being film stars. The big dog stares at me,
as if asking why he isn't enough. I look past
him for the squirrels but they are scooting up
two separate pines, while the lake looks on,
wondering what on earth I am bothered by.
Yeah, as if it hasn't drowned enough people.

I walk down to chuck a stone into the water,
to punish the lake. It is alive. Have those squirrels
ever swum in it? Have the Chippewa ever valued
grilling and eating them? I know the mountain-
men eat squirrels in rural Tennessee, but this
place is lake-haunted, and a different law
rules here. I waltz back to the porch, glass
of red wine in my hand, but the squirrels are

no longer visible, sleeping, no doubt, under the
trees they run up in daylight. Not even a chipmunk
shows his little face. Beyond the porch, the lake
shines in the moonlight, and hisses an invitation
for me to strip off and go for a swim in it. I know
now what it's about. A Chippewa, long dead, who'd
been called *Black Squirrel* must have drowned here
and is begging me to jump in and join him.

# The Bone Rosary

The big dog's grave is already dug, a few
yards from the lake, and all the bones he's
sucked the marrow from are strung on a rope
draped over the porch railing, a bone rosary,
waiting to be hooked to a rusty chain hung
from a metal post stuck in the ground, poking
out over the water. I can already imagine
the reactions of people in boats who'll pass,
what they'll think of the resident of the house.
There might be more to tickle their fancy –
I have a BB gun and ball bearings in a cupboard
that would kill as many black squirrels as I
wanted. And I might just commission a black
totem pole. And although there are no records
of anyone walking on the waters of Mullett Lake,
I think I may visit a hypnotist in Harbor Springs
to see if she can facilitate this. I'd love to run out
into the middle of the lake, carrying the Stars
and Stripes, and make all the folk in boats
I meet faint and fall into the water, maybe to
drown there, and befriend the big dog's ghost.

## The Bear

Whenever I turned the TV on I found Trump,
not yet President. There he was, towering,
pointing a finger, haranguing me, always dressed
in the same garb – blue blazer, white shirt,
red tie – like a bear with the star-spangled-banner
draped on him. Yes, that's what he was, a bear –
just like those that had prowled through the lake-
side forests in northern Michigan where I was.
How many salmon and trout had they gobbled,
after spearing them on those sharp claws?
The American people probably resembled big
fish to Trump, especially those who voted Democrat.
Ah, how he must have enjoyed pronging them.
Those Chippewa, however, would have been
pretty adept at snagging bears, then killing them,
skinning them, hacking them into chunks of meat
to sell in the settlements of Petoskey, Cheboygan
and others that have long since disappeared,
along with the old native recipes for cooking bear.
I felt like going to the nearest reservation to see
if someone could contact an ancestor to obtain
some details for me – I'd pay them well, and I'd
buy some illicit bear-meat from them, too, then
I'd get busy in the kitchen, or outside on the grill,
and I'd sit chomping in front of Trump onscreen.
Oh yeah, that's what I wanted to do back then,
while the whole scenario was unfolding, as if it
would have made any damned difference at all!

# The Oarlock

I found the oarlock in the lake, close to the shore.
It was lying there in two dozen inches of water.

I waded in to retrieve it, then plonked it on the desk
while I changed my soaking jeans for a dry pair.

I held the oarlock under a light. There was no rust,
or any other discolouring. It was smooth as a pearl.

How long had it been since it had encountered air?
No one rowed here now. There were only motor-boats.

The last person to row using that oarlock as a fulcrum
couldn't have a scrap of flesh left on his buried bones.

Why was it lying there on the lake-bed waiting for me?
Had there been an accident? Had the boat gone down?

Maybe a succession of storms had done for the wood
and buried the other oarlock in the sandy bottom,

leaving this one fated to become my souvenir
of life and death in Mullett Lake when I'm back home.

## Spooked

The lake is shiny today, as if the light, on its way
here from the sun, bounced off three moons.
Whatever it is, there's a glow that's unnatural,
that makes the water wriggle, and paints
the stagnant grass, the fallen, brittle leaves.
The squirrels are clearly spooked and stay put.
They're right, I think. No good can come of it.

And yet, boats are out. I go down to the water
and count eight, no less, including one speeder
trying to set a new world record. I walk out onto
the jetty to follow it better, and the structure starts
shaking, as if it wants to toss me into the lake.
I hear a deep gurgle beneath me as I inch back.
The Stars and Stripes hangs limp atop its pole.

# The Old Xmas Tree

The old Xmas tree is gone,
it lay in the corner of the garden
like the corpse of a soldier
from mid January to mid June
getting paler by the day, by
the week, like a drying seaweed.
I wanted to bring it in again
and set it up, where it used to be,
in front of the window, blocking
the TV, soaking up the music
that flowed around it and maybe
through it, though I didn't
know how porous its brown leaves
or needles remained. I went
away, leaving it there, and a man
came to cut the grass, and remove
the cuttings and the petrified tree.
It was like a fallen statue had been
taken away, one the blackbird
had often sat on and sung to me from.
I lay down where it had been
and I slept, to dream of Xmas,
the presents placed under me,
the gonks, cards and angels in my
branches, and me green again.

# Double Dirge

The owl rose above the dead dog
and hooted a five-blast nightbird dirge
but the only creature that heard it
was the wasp that had stung the dog
and would expire before the morning.

Unknown to any of the above crowd
a deaf boy with a luminous crossbow
and perfect night-vision was taking aim
on the circling owl and unloosed a
red-tipped arrow into the tan feathers

beneath the big eyes whose owner
dropped like a falling angel onto the
corpse of the dog, while the feral boy
swapped his crossbow for a fiddle,
and played a double dirge to the forest.

# Owl Song

The four candles took a while to burn down
but they did, leaving the boy's corpse in the dark,
apart from a blue light filched from the hospital
that wouldn't have lit a weasel's way home.

The boy's father was on top of the water-tower
with a whisky-bottle. His mother was a kilometre
out into the Mediterranean under the moon
and was finally, finally, thinking of turning back.

Only the boy's sister was in the house with him
and she was sleepwalking up the steep stairs
to stand at his feet and shout out in her sleep
the old song he'd loved so much about the owls.

# The Yellow Pole

Paint the pole yellow,
stick it in the grave
of a poet, but make sure
the poet's lying there.

Bring some new jazz
to the ceremony (maybe
German), and French wine,
a case of twelve, at least.

At the stroke of noon,
produce from your rucksack
the white snake, and the
red lizard, and allow them

to climb up the yellow pole,
the snake last, and both
to sit there, like the flag
of poetry, or of existence.

Have a youthful friend
film it on her iPhone, and
tweet it everywhere,
while a toast to the poet

goes viral, and the bottles
empty, and you return
the snake and the lizard
to the silver rucksack,

pull out the yellow pole,
march to the swollen river,
arch your arm and fire the
lemon javelin into the water.